# Being Your Own Superstar

## How to Expand Your **Love** Capacity

JOIE GHARRITY

Being Your Own Superstar
Joie Gharrity

Being Your Own Superstar—How to Expand Your Love Capacity



ISBN: 978-1-7351638-9-5 (Print)

ISBN: 979-8-9856099-0-5 (Digital)



For information regarding permission, write to:

The Zebra Ink
PO Box 16664
Rocky River, OH 44116
publisher@thezebraink.com

www.thezebraink.com

Printed in the United States of America

Copyeditor: The Zebra Ink
Cover Design: Heather Robison
Interior Formatting: Voices in Print

Order additional copies of this book today on Amazon.com

10 9 8 7 6 5 4 3 2 1

# Contents

Dear Dad,

Thank you for encouraging me to draw outside the lines, and for teaching me to never define myself by other people's standards. It is because of you I have the courage to step up to the plate and keep swinging until I hit one out of the park. I offer a special thank you for reminding me over the years to not fall into the trap of chasing the Golden Circle and helping me see I am the Golden Circle.

I am so very proud to be your daughter.

# Being Your Own *Superstar*

## How to Expand Your **Love** Capacity

Being Your Own Superstar
Joie Gharrity

# Welcome Superstar!

You are going to be so glad you picked up this book!

**THERE WAS A TIME** in my life when I felt frustrated and tired. I worked so hard to make my dreams and desires come true, yet they always seemed out of reach. You might feel that way too. Are you looking for the secret sauce to make your dreams come to fruition? You need not look any further than right here, on these pages.

The key to getting all that you want in life is probably not what you think it is. I know I didn't think this *one thing* had anything to do with it. What is the *one thing* that will unlock all of your wants and wishes? It is LOVE!

I can't even tell you how skeptical I was in the beginning. How could love—what I thought was just romance and relationships—have anything to do with my success? This book will detail how love, does indeed, has everything to do with it.

Truth is…I am not a super affectionate person. I am not big on giving or receiving hugs. I am not sentimental. I did not grow up a flower child. I never bought into Hallmark cards. Valentine's Day was not my favorite holiday.

Growing up I would hear things like, "All you will ever need is love." "Love is the answer." Honestly, I never thought that love had anything to do with gaining more success or making my dreams and desires come to fruition. Instead, I fully bought into it coming down to being driven, working myself into the ground, and getting that lucky break along the way.

It never occurred to me that Love had everything to do with success until three years ago at my friend's life celebration. I was feeling blue and not inspired and I asked myself the age-old question "What is life all about?" Then something extraordinary happened at that very moment. It was as if a bright light of pure love washed over me. A series of memories flooded my consciousness. Each memory connected a dot…

Read on to learn what I downloaded as each memory connected those dots, one to the next, and how I learned that luck has nothing to do with dreams and desires coming true. I share the reason you play small isn't solely because of the fear of criticism or rejection and buying into being driven and working yourself into the ground…is chasing what I call the GOLDEN CIRCLE. That CHASE is what keeps your dreams and desires from coming to fruition. I also share activities that move you towards growing what I have coined your LOVE CAPACITY or LC for short, along with the Expand your LOVE CAPACITY DAILY HABITS SYSTEM LEVEL 1, which takes only thirty minutes a day. I share my LOVE CAPACITY journey with you and how both my personal and professional life have changed in the most extraordinary ways.

Thank you for joining me on the
journey of a lifetime.
Let's begin!

# The Golden Circle

## *And so, it begins ...*

**I WAS BORN TO** a bartender, Dennis Gharrity, the son of a factory worker, and Berta Nunez-Gharrity, daughter of a copper miner, in a small apartment in San Francisco. My parents were young, happy, and excited about me, their firstborn. We didn't have much, but there was never a need or want in our household. My family had a large network in the community, including chefs, maître-d's, restaurant owners, and people in the service industries who all took care of each other like an extended family. It never felt like I was without, but after applying to an elite high school in San Francisco, I received quite an introduction to the GOLDEN CIRCLE.

I'll never forget the day I was accepted into the coveted school in the heart of San Francisco and exposed to a new class system. the GOLDEN CIRCLE was an echelon of girls who came from families with well-known last names and parents who lived in prestigious locations and had economic power.

I found a world where identities were based inside the GOLDEN CIRCLE OF INFLUENCE—where society grants famous last names and affluence an apparent birthright. I discovered the GOLDEN CIRCLE is a class system that is perpetuated through family connections and wealth, which has long been indoctrinated throughout our worldwide society. It's based on last name, vocation, and more importantly—wealth.

Being on the outside of the GOLDEN CIRCLE (GC) OF INFLUENCE, I quickly picked up the signals of somehow not being as worthy. Even at the beginning of high school, not being born into the GOLDEN CIRCLE fostered deep feelings of insecurity which played on my self-worth. I was determined to get into the GC, thinking, *if I work hard enough and sacrifice enough, somehow, I will be granted access.*

I still felt the lack of worth and insecurity when I found myself working in Hollywood in my early twenties. I worked for a production company that had just landed a big deal for their first movie and granted office space in the famous Carocol Building on Sunset Boulevard, along with other top-level production companies. One would think that I had made it into the GOLDEN CIRCLE, but once again, I just found myself on the outside, amongst an elite community of Hollywood famous last names, who lived in prestigious locations and had economic power. I immediately picked up the signals which played on my self-worth.

So even working in Hollywood wasn't enough ...

Chasing the GC had me buy fully into the belief that being successful all comes down to being driven, working hard, and getting a lucky break somewhere along the way. It disempowered me and it does the same to you.

Were you born outside of the Golden Circle? The signals are powerful; however, they've become so ingrained in society it is not unusual to unconsciously react to the signs. I didn't connect the dots until I started my LOVE CAPACITY journey. Today, I can confidently share with you that there is a higher truth.

Every person, no matter what last name, location, gender, or economic power they were born into, is a child of The Divine with a unique purpose, gifts, and talents.

The GOLDEN CIRCLE indicator is little more than a man-made barrier between you and your birthright.

It is your birthright to embrace your life purpose, to stand in the purposeful vocation that brings you joy, to grow your Love Capacity, and to have your dreams and desires come to fruition.

Embracing your true birthright and expanding your capacity to allow, receive, and accept massive amounts of love is the game-changing practice I feel passionately called to share with you. I know it works; I've personally seen what a tremendous difference it has made in my life and others.

Until a few years ago, when I was sitting at my friend's celebration of life, it never occurred **to me** that love had anything to do with my success. I was feeling blue and uninspired, asking "What is life all about?"

# What Does Love Have to Do with It?

**GROWING UP I NEVER** thought that love had anything to do with gaining more success nor making my dreams and desires come to fruition. Instead, I chased THE GOLDEN CIRCLE which in turn made me very driven, working myself into the ground, and hoping to get that lucky break along the way. The drive came from chasing the GOLDEN CIRCLE. I bought into the belief system which has long been indoctrinated into society—that value is based on last name, vocation, and more importantly wealth.

Until a few years ago, when I was sitting at my friend's celebration of life, it never occurred to me that love had anything to do with my success. I was feeling blue and uninspired, asking "What is life all about?" Losing another friend, not being sure that I was on the right career path, still not being in a meaningful romantic relationship, and questioning why I worked in the Hollywood entertainment business for most of my adult life were definitely pain points for me that day.

Then, at that moment, something extraordinary happened. It was as if a bright light of pure love washed over me. Within seconds, a series of memories flooded my consciousness.

The series of memories connected the dots and answered the questions I was pondering that day. Each memory I recalled shed a brighter light on my bigger why and the real reason why I remained in the Hollywood entertainment industry for fifteen-plus years. My *chasing* the GOLDEN CIRCLE made sense. There were memories I hadn't thought of in years, but when they flooded in, all I could see was how each memory drove toward one common theme.

*I am the Golden Circle.*

The love I felt at that moment was powerful and empowering. It lifted me from feeling hopeless to finding hope.

All the memories downloaded that day were memories to which I had never given much thought. I recalled the first movie premiere I attended at the start of my Hollywood career. I was so impressed by how at ease the superstars were on the red carpet, faced with countless screaming fans always showering them with adoration.

Then I recalled a superstar sitting down at a piano in the middle of a five-star hotel in New York City and playing it beautifully. The piano was in the middle of the long hallway to the room elevators. It was clearly just for decorative purposes. Customers in the lobby heard the music and once they realized who was playing, they surrounded him, showing their admiration as he played. I remember how surprised I was that he didn't double guess himself by asking for permission to play the piano and was comfortable allowing others to show up to celebrate his talent.

The next memory was of one night I saw a star standing alone in the hotel roundabout waiting for her significant other, who was the lead actor I had been working with that day, to return from the movie set. It was rare to see a superstar without an entourage. I remember I was in awe at how at ease she was in her body, and it was obvious she was living life in the moment.

There was also the memory of a Hollywood movie director leaving for a studio meeting to pitch his next movie. That movie had a price tag of one hundred million dollars he had to raise if he was going to make it. I remember how amazed I was by his drive and passion and his ability to accept one hundred million dollars with ease and grace.

The next memory was about traveling to Japan with my boss who was a Hollywood movie director. He was to meet with a major studio about directing the sequel of a classic globally recognized film. This film literally was engrained in the Japanese culture and beyond. His agents warned him it was a long shot that the studio would grant him the green light. I recall thinking how courageous his unwavering determination was to share his passion and vision for the film he had been a fan of since childhood. To the surprise of many, he was given the green light.

The next glimpse really started to help me see the common theme of all these memories. At a friend's birthday party, I met a talent manager who told me about a rising star in the music industry. I was interested in learning more about her and meeting her. I saw her perform at a famous venue on Sunset Boulevard and even though the attendance was moderate, she performed as if it was a packed house. I remember thinking how inspired I was at how she shared her gifts and talents with pure enthusiasm, not getting caught up in the numbers, and instead, embracing the moment. Shortly after that encounter, she became a globally recognized superstar.

The final memory was of a time when I was watching the Academy Awards. A team I worked with on a blockbuster movie was nominated in their category. They won. I was impressed by their ease as they celebrated their success on stage in front of millions of viewers worldwide.

That day at my friend's life celebration as one memory connected to the next and the next, the ultimate aha moment illuminated itself. The truth was that we are all intended to allow, receive, and accept love. I saw how the superstars have mastered the ability to allow, receive and accept massive amounts of love. That is why they have so much ease and grace when accepting adoration, gifts, and recognition. They have filled their capacity to receive monumental proportions of love.

It became obvious that the reason we play small isn't solely because of the fear of criticism or rejection which I always believed was the bottom-line. Yes, that does play a part in the equation. However, the secret sauce downloaded to me that day is that the reason we play small is because of our inability to allow, receive and accept LOVE. The superstars and leaders in the industry I observed could allow, receive, and accept massive amounts of love. The more love you can allow, receive, and accept, the bigger the dreams and desires you have can come to fruition.

As I reflected on my memories it dawned on me how society doesn't teach us to take in massive amounts of love daily. Media encourages us to strive for the impossible. Perfect lifestyles and body types are celebrated, and imperfections of any kind are shameful and need to be corrected. I am a huge fan of educators and education. However, it occurred to me that even when you receive an A on a report card or assignment there is a prevailing question about why you didn't get an A+. It got me thinking about how failure is graded, scored, and ridiculed. That even when you do get over one finish line the typical question is, "What's next?" The amount of negativity and lack of celebration bestowed on us daily from so many directions becomes the focus…the norm. Allowing, receiving, and accepting massive amounts of love is not revered or taught.

I believe that several of the superstars and industry leaders I had observed over that fifteen-plus years working in the Hollywood entertainment industry have discovered the secret sauce of growing what I call their LOVE CAPACITY to massive levels—to the Grand Canyon level!

What do I mean by Love Capacity? Every person has a capacity to allow, receive and accept love. The size of your LOVE CAPACITY is in direct alignment with your capacity to allow your dreams and desires to come to fruition.

Dreams, desires, money, awards, and material things…all are just love showing up in different forms. Getting what you want has to do with allowing, receiving, and accepting love. If your dreams and desires are coming up short you will want to grow your LOVE CAPACITY (or LC) because it is in direct alignment.

---

Their Love Capacity was in alignment to allow, receive, and accept love in the form of adoration, gifts, and recognition.

---

When I observed the superstar sitting down at a piano in the middle of a five-star hotel, without double guessing himself by asking for permission and shrinking when others showed up to celebrate him...

---

His Love Capacity was in alignment to allow, receive, and accept love in the form of
being celebrated.

---

The time I observed a superstar standing at the hotel roundabout, at ease without her entourage waiting for her significant other ...

---

Her Love Capacity was in alignment to allow, receive, and accept love in the form of being at ease in her body and living life in the moment.

---

Another instance was my observation of a Hollywood movie director leaving for a studio meeting to pitch his next movie with a price tag of one hundred million dollars, which he received with ease and grace...

---

His Love Capacity was in alignment to allow, receive, and accept love in the form of one hundred million dollars.

---

When I observed a Hollywood movie director pitching the sequel of a classic globally recognized film...

---

His Love Capacity was in alignment to allow, receive, and accept love in the form of getting the movie funded and his dream coming to fruition.

---

In another observation of an up-and-coming superstar sharing her gifts and talents with pure enthusiasm to a moderately filled room...

---

Her Love Capacity was in alignment to allow, receive, and accept love in the form of enthusiasm for her gifts and

talents that eventually made
her a star.

---

In the final instance, when I observed friends accepting an Oscar on stage and how impressed I was at their ease as they celebrated their success on stage in front of millions of viewers worldwide ...

---

Their Love Capacity was in alignment to allow, receive, and accept love in the form of an Oscar.

---

You might be thinking "Well those people are famous so of course..." And I am telling you it has nothing to do with fame or Hollywood. People you admire for their success, influence, opportunities, fame, wealth are not necessarily more talented nor gifted than you. They just have grown their LOVE CAPACITY to match their dreams and desires. I want to make sure that you also know that no one grows their LC overnight. It takes time. But it is so worth it!

When our dreams and desires come up short or **not at all**, it is common for negative emotions like disappointment, anger, or regret to take up precious Love Capacity.

# My Rebirth

**THE DAY AT MY FRIEND'S** life celebration was my rebirth. I said, "yes" to spreading the word that LOVE has everything to do with success. That your LOVE CAPACITY is the key to you making your dreams and desires come to fruition.

As I started my LOVE CAPACITY journey, I realized that I had to first, start with quieting the Golden Circle signals. The signals that our value is based on last name and vocation, but more importantly, wealth. The Golden Circle is a series of signals that distracts and encourages us to believe being driven, working yourself into the ground, and luck have something to do with our dreams and desires coming to fruition. More importantly, the signals encourage us to chase the Golden Circle to be granted access to those dreams and desires. When our dreams and desires come up short or not at all, it is common for negative emotions like disappointment, anger, or regret to take up precious Love Capacity. If I was going to grow my LC to massive levels, I would have to stop *chasing* the Golden Circle and remember that I am the Golden Circle.

Next, I knew that I had to create a daily practice and the Expand Your Love Capacity Daily Habits System was born. I designed this book to double as a guide and I share the Expand Your Love Capacity Daily Habits System Level 1 with you so you can kick start growing your Love Capacity today. In the EXPAND YOUR LOVE CAPACITY DAILY HABITS SYSTEM, I share how to quiet the Golden Circle signals. I also share how to replace negative emotions taking up precious Love Capacity, with massive amounts of love, and how to grow your LC to align with your dreams and desires. You can design your life in the most extraordinary ways.

> The great news is that you can grow your Love Capacity. It does not take a special set of talents and has nothing to do with your gender, ethnicity, or vocation.

I want to be clear that your religious beliefs are none of my business. This book is not to push a religious belief. I do refer to The Divine in the book; however, you can refer to your God, Higher Power, Source, or what feels most comfortable for you. This book is created to share the ultimate secret sauce that love has everything to do with you getting what you want.

The great news is that you can grow your LOVE CAPACITY. It does not take a special set of talents and has nothing to do with your gender, ethnicity, or vocation.

If you follow the teachings I lay out in the EXPAND YOUR LOVE CAPACITY DAILY HABITS SYSTEM LEVEL 1, you will also be inspired to take action and accelerate forward-motion daily. Be sure not to skip over any step or action hoping to find a shortcut. Finish each step—in order.

As we take the LC journey together and you begin the EXPAND YOUR CAPACITY DAILY HABITS SYSTEM, small and big wins will start to drop in because you are growing your LC. What might seem like random coincidences or chance opportunities…absolutely are not. They are in direct alignment to your LOVE CAPACITY'S ability to allow, receive, and accept.

I am so glad we are about to begin the journey of building your capacity to allow, receive, and accept as much love as you desire.

I had walked away from my inner game practices several years before. Now, with nothing to lean on, my vibrations hit an all-time low and everything in the world looked grey.

> I had walked away from my inner game practices several years before. Now, with nothing to lean on, my vibrations hit an all-time low and everything in the world looked grey.

# Best Kept Secret

*Two decades ago...*

**One day I was** invited to a studio lot to visit with a famous composer who was recording an upcoming movie track. At the end of the day, I remember thinking that life was pure magic.

That night, before I rested my head on my pillow and closed my eyes, I knew in my gut that something big was about to happen. I assumed that one of my dreams or desires would become a reality. Instead, at midnight my phone rang, and it was my mom. She was sobbing. My brother passed away suddenly in a car accident while working on a film in Wyoming. My entire world came crashing down. My brother and I were only fourteen months apart. We were what people refer to as Irish twins. Both our personal and professional worlds were tightly intertwined. I immediately felt responsible since I was instrumental in getting him a career in the movie industry.

I had walked away from my inner game practices several years before. Now, with nothing to lean on, my vibrations hit an all-time low and everything in the world looked grey. I was still working in the Hollywood entertainment business; however, the Golden Circle signal had gotten loud, and my self-value completely crashed and burned.

I awoke daily, struggling and suffering from deep depression. I went down some dark rabbit holes. I was desperate to feel better even just a little.

One afternoon I turned to an inner game tool I had learned from my meditation teacher years before moving to LA. I closed my eyes and began to do a simple breathing exercise. After ten minutes I could feel my body begin to relax into each breath. I felt a calm come over my body I hadn't experienced in years.

After about twenty minutes I felt a strong presence of love. It was so strong that I remember feeling scared and just as I was about to stop the breathing exercise, I saw Jesus standing in front of me. He radiated pure love and grace. He moved towards me and then embraced me. Love washed over my body and into my heart. It was incredible to receive so much love. I was surprised by the encounter. I had heard the stories about Jesus in church growing up, but I had no emotional connection to him. I certainly didn't consider myself religious. I was attracted to spirituality but never to a religious practice or church.

That day I knew that I had been given a huge gift. I knew this was the first step towards me releasing myself from a self-made internal purgatory.

A few weeks later I decided to try the breathing exercise again, hoping I would encounter Jesus once more. I wanted to feel that overwhelming love. Instead of Jesus, this time it was the Virgin Mary wrapped in roses who showered me with massive amounts of love. Again, I was surprised and elated by the encounter. The love was massive and filled my heart with joy.

I told only one person about the two encounters for fear of being judged. I called my meditation teacher who I studied with in the Bay Area. She immediately believed me and asked me to pack my things and leave Hollywood for good. She wanted me to return home and to allow her to mentor me. At the time that was a tall order. I was obsessed with *chasing* the GOLDEN CIRCLE and working in the Hollywood entertainment industry was my best bet. I flat-out refused her offer. I vowed to keep my secret and not tell another living soul. Until now. I wrestled with sharing my experience with you. However, since being on my LC journey I realized that the encounters with Jesus and Mary showering me with a massive amount of love over two decades ago were the first step to getting out of the self-made purgatory of shame, guilt, regret, and sadness that was taking up precious LOVE CAPACITY. It was also the entry point to spreading the word that love has everything to do with it.

As I read the article, a memory of my brother washed over me. While working in Hollywood together before his passing he would tell me and his friends often to "Spread the love." and "It is all about the love."

...a memory of my brother washed over me. While working in Hollywood together before his passing he would tell me and his friends often to
"Spread the love."
and
"It is all about the love."

# To Love and Be Loved

## *Your dreams and desires are waiting patiently...*

**ON LIFE'S JOURNEY, THERE** are many setups. Just like in Hollywood, every good script sets the audience up for the premise. Life is no different.

A few years ago, I was traveling back to San Francisco from Seattle, Washington when I read an article that was the prelude to the download I got during my friend's celebration of life. It was about the power of love. As I read the article, a memory of my brother washed over me. While working in Hollywood together before his passing he would tell me and his friends often to "Spread the love." and "It is all about the love."

It got me thinking about my capacity to love and my willingness to allow love in. I asked myself the question and heard my internal voice scream *Gavin passed away tragically. It is not safe to be loved or to love.* I hadn't connected the dots until that moment. And I realized that I had kept all my serious relationships after my brother's passing at bay. Internally I wasn't willing to commit. It was a hard truth to face. My internal story had been affecting my capacity for love for so long, and I didn't even know it.

That next year I turned fifty and rented a home in San Diego to celebrate with my friends. Before my friends arrived for the celebration, I sat on the rooftop deck and watched the sunset. I was at ease, and I heard my internal voice whisper, *you are ready to allow yourself to love and to be loved.* At that moment I said yes without hesitation. I set an intention I would commit to being open to love. However, I knew there would be plenty of inner game work that would have to be done first. I set the intention to allow, receive, and accept love and I had no idea how I was going to do that.

Six months following my friend's life celebration I designed the EXPAND YOUR LOVE CAPACITY DAILY HABITS and started my LOVE CAPACITY JOURNEY. Being disciplined, I practiced the EXPAND YOUR LOVE CAPACITY DAILY HABITS seven days a week. At the start of my journey, my LC was full of disappointment, regret, shame, guilt, sadness. As my LC grew, the negative emotions that were taking up precious capacity started to move out and were replaced with massive amounts of love.

This brings me to some exciting news. Dreams and desires you have put on the back burner for years, even have forgotten about, could potentially come to fruition once your LC starts growing. It can be something small, medium, or big. It has happened to me.

For instance, over twenty years ago I was watching a music award show. An up-and-coming artist took center stage. I was hypnotized by his talent, and I remember how eager I was to see him in concert. Sadly, the opportunity never presented itself. I had totally forgotten about that desire until I was offered a VIP ticket to see him in concert just this year. I immediately said yes to the opportunity without hesitation. You might be thinking that is just a random coincidence or chance opportunity. There is no such thing. Nothing is by chance nor random. And you might be thinking well that is no big deal, it is just a concert. However, it was a big deal because I was able to connect the dots. It was proof that my LC was growing and pulling in a desire from my past I gave up on, even kicked to the curb, but because my LC was in alignment, it came to fruition.

For instance, I had seen a luxurious accessory worn by a star on a TV show and I was eager to have one because it was chic and cool. However, I knew that it had a heavy price tag on it, and I immediately dismissed it. I never mentioned the desire to anyone. During the holidays, this year my husband surprised me with that exact accessory. I was surprised by the gift for two reasons. One, the price tag was not a typical purchase, and two, I had never even dropped a hint. As I sat with my gift, I realized that it was my LC. That desire was in alignment and therefore it came to fruition.

I want to be clear—I do not believe in magic or hocus pocus. I do believe that we are powerful beings. When you incorporate the right tools in a daily practice like the EXPAND YOUR LOVE CAPACITY DAILY HABITS SYSTEM, your LOVE CAPACITY opens to allow, receive, and accept massive amounts of love. Then dreams and desires of all sizes begin to show up in the most extraordinary ways.

Remember how I set an intention I would commit to being open to love? Just three months after starting the EXPAND YOUR LOVE CAPACITY DAILY HABITS SYSTEM AND growing my LC, I met the love of my life. One year later my dream of getting engaged became a reality. One year after that, my dream of getting married to Roger Moore came true.

...since growing my LC with the expand your love capacity daily habits system, my entire life, both personally and professionally, changed in the most extraordinary ways.

# In Just Three Years

*My entire life changed in the best of ways...*

**IN THE THREE YEARS** since growing my LC with the EXPAND YOUR LOVE CAPACITY DAILY HABITS SYSTEM, my entire life, both personally and professionally, changed in the most extraordinary ways.

As I mentioned I had become a serial dater in my forties and into my fifties. I had lost all hope of meeting someone that would be compatible to spend the rest of my life with. Just three months after starting the EXPAND YOUR LOVE CAPACITY DAILY HABITS SYSTEM and growing my LC, I met the love of my life. One year later my dream of getting engaged came true. The year following that, my dream of getting married to Roger Moore was actualized. Though my dad's health was failing, my desire to have my dad attend the ceremony was fulfilled.

After returning to The Bay Area from Hollywood (where I moved to for a second time when a start-up that hired me closed its doors), I was determined to never work for anyone else again. So, I committed to 113 Branding, a company focused on gaining more visibility and influence in the marketplace for entrepreneurs and creative types. I also became an international speaker. As committed as I was, I quickly discovered how difficult running your own business could be, and though my business would thrive for a while, it would suddenly slow down. I felt I was always on a stop-and-go rollercoaster. Since that day at my friend's celebration and practicing the EXPAND YOUR LOVE CAPACITY DAILY HABITS for just one year, I got off the stop-and-go rollercoaster, and my dream of creating a successful and sustainable business became my new reality. It also happened during Covid, one of the most difficult times in business history. What is even more extraordinary is that I renamed my company brand to Joie G 113 and stepped fully into my spotlight.

For my entire professional career, I stayed in the shadows. I was always helping others stand in their spotlight. Being the center of attention was difficult for me. I would feel great uneasiness when approached with an opportunity to be spotlighted. Almost immediately after starting the Expand Your Love Capacity Daily Habits System my dream came true. I wanted to step out of the shadows and stand in a large spotlight, shining a bright light on my gifts and talents. That dream came to fruition as evidenced by being consistently asked to be a featured guest on podcasts, live shows, summits, and panels. What is even more extraordinary is that I say yes to each opportunity without hesitation.

Writing my first book, *The Red Carpet Guide to Visibility and Influence,* was exciting as was becoming an accomplished author. However, writing a book takes a ton of time and energy. I knew that I wanted to write a second book on what was downloaded to me that day at my friend's life celebration to share the secret sauce with the world. I had little to no enthusiasm to write it though. It took practicing a year of the EXPAND YOUR LOVE CAPACITY DAILY HABITS SYSTEM before I was re-energized enough to pursue it. My enthusiasm soared higher and higher. My dream of writing a second book, which you are reading now, came to fruition. What is even more extraordinary is that I dedicated the book to my dad and got to read him the dedication before his passing. It is a moment with my dad I will never forget.

> What is even more extraordinary is that I dedicated the book to my dad and got to read him the dedication before his passing. It is a moment with my dad I will never forget.

The day I turned fifty, I was sitting on the rooftop patio of a gorgeous beach house in Mission Beach, California when I dreamed of stepping into my own spotlight and being recognized as a talent. Three years after starting the EXPAND YOUR LOVE CAPACITY DAILY HABITS SYSTEM my dream of recognition as talent was complete. At the end of 2021, I was signed to a reputable podcast talent agency out of Los Angeles.

My chasing the GOLDEN CIRCLE since high school played negatively on my self-value and that caused me to not be at ease in my body or with my body. Quieting the GOLDEN CIRCLE signals and releasing negative emotions, which had been taking up precious capacity, allowed my desire to be more at ease daily in my body come to fruition as well. This is extraordinary in so many ways. I never thought in my lifetime I could quiet the internal negative talk. I still struggle at times with it, but it is night and day from what I experienced before I started building my LC.

I was at a retreat and the moderator walked us through a meditation exercise of visualizing a place where we'd feel most comfortable in the future. I saw myself in a gorgeous, customized living space. I loved the space and I turned it into a desire. At the time that space felt so out of reach. I tucked it away on the back burner along with so many desires I had placed on countless vision boards over the years. Fast forward three years after starting the EXPAND YOUR LOVE CAPACITY DAILY HABITS SYSTEM my desire came to fruition. I was gifted a gorgeous living space that was customized just for me.

Now it is your turn to get what you want.

# How To Get What You Want

**THE SYSTEM LEVEL 1** is divided into two sections. Section One is the EXPAND YOUR LOVE CAPACITY DAILY HABITS ACTIVITY SECTION, which will help you:

Identify when you have chased the Golden Circle.

Recognize what negative emotions are taking up LC capacity.

Release and forgive the past.

Get clear on just three dreams and desires to start with so you can assign the virtual love notes.

Each step is critical to setting you up for success in Section Two the EXPAND YOUR LOVE CAPACITY DAILY HABITS. *The best part of Level I is that it takes only thirty minutes per day.*

I am a big fan of dream and desire setting. However, the EXPAND YOUR LOVE CAPACITY DAILY HABITS DREAM and DESIRE SETTING ACTIVITY turns traditional goal setting on its head! The traditional way to set goals is to focus on all the steps you need to take in order to move towards the outcome. In the EXPAND YOUR LOVE CAPACITY DAILY HABITS SYSTEM, you create a list of dreams and desires. Once you get clear on your dreams and desires, you will move them to the side.

Here is the thing: it is important to get clear—very clear—on the dream or desire, but if you get caught up in the details without making sure that your Love Capacity is in alignment with them, you'll find you're going in the back door.

In the EXPAND YOUR LOVE CAPACITY DAILY HABITS GOAL SETTING ACTIVITY, I share the importance of growing your LOVE CAPACITY to align with the dreams and desires as being your top priority. If your LC is not in alignment, and the dream and desire are not in alignment, then it is very possible that as they fall short of your expectations, disappointment, regret, and frustration will take up precious LOVE CAPACITY. Or the outcome may show up in what I call a stop-and-go scenario where you will experience some evidence of the dream or desire coming true but then it doesn't fully appear. And even worse—if your LC isn't large enough to align with your dream or desire, it may come to fruition but over time you cannot sustain it.

Let's talk about love notes...

In EXPAND YOUR LOVE CAPACITY DAILY HABITS ACTIVITY SECTION I ask you to put how many Love Notes per individual dream or desire it would take to obtain it. When I refer to love notes I mean *virtual love notes*—a note that showers you with love. Human beings need a tangible number on which to focus. It helps you to wrap your head around how much love it will really take to get what you want.

When I assign a number of love notes next to my dream or desire, I visualize each individual love note the size of a piece of confetti. I was recently at a concert and the performer had confetti shower us at the end of his performance. I visualized each piece of confetti as a love note that evening. It helped me to visualize countless love notes. I encourage you to do the same.

As you assign how many love notes per each dream or desire, you create an emotional connection to them. I also have you then put your dreams and desires to the side, so you don't get lost in the details. WHY? Because endless details are your way of trying to control the outcome. And that is sabotage. Instead, I want you to just grow your LC. It will be mind-blowing how your dreams or desires show up when you allow, receive, and accept love.

My hope is that you will have the same aha that I had when I started my LC journey. Once I authentically assigned a number of love notes per a dream or desire, I was able to genuinely recognize how much love I would have to allow, receive, and accept. It was also liberating because now I was able to take the mystery out of why some dreams or desires were not showing up at all or coming up short. It put me in the driver's seat. No more wishing or hoping. I now know my number one activity is to keep growing my LC.

How do you decide on how many virtual love notes per dream or desire? Let's say one of your dreams is that you want to earn a million dollars. Why shouldn't you have what you want? It is your birthright. In this very moment could you allow, receive, and accept a million virtual love notes? Remember, money is just love in a different form. What if someone right now walked up to you and handed you a million-dollar check? Would you shrink or would you take the check without hesitation? And if you did take it without hesitation, would you begin to worry, which is a negative emotion that takes up precious LC, about the responsibilities that came along with that million-dollar check? Remember negative emotions that take up precious LC are roadblocks to your dreams and desires. That is why it is important to grow your LC muscle. Perhaps you start with ten, twenty, one-hundred thousand love notes. In time you will feel at ease with one-million love notes/dollars.

Let's say you want to quit your job and travel the world. How big would your Love Capacity have to be to allow, receive and accept that dream to come to fruition? How many love notes would you need in order for you to fully embrace your dream of quitting your job, traveling the world to take your dream from feeling like a fantasy to reality? Again, perhaps you start by allowing, receiving, and accepting ten thousand, thirty thousand...love notes and grow your LC muscle. As it gets stronger your dream will feel less like a fantasy and doable.

What if you are an author that wants to sell a million books? Could you allow, receive, and accept a million love notes? Sales are just love in a different form. Could you allow strangers globally to send you a love note in the form of buying your book? And what about the responsibilities of being the center of attention? Anyone that sells a million copies of their book would have to be on endless media and have fans that shower them with adoration. Would you lean in without hesitation or would you shrink a little from the picture I just painted for you? If that picture feels overwhelming, then perhaps you start with a thousand, ten-thousand, fifty-thousand love notes and so on. As your LC muscle gets stronger, so will your ease with selling one-million books.

What if your dream is to own a mansion and the mansion is worth three million dollars? Now visualize receiving three-million virtual love notes. That is a lot of virtual love notes coming at you all at once. However, being aware of the number of love notes has gotten you closer to your dream home because now you know how big you need to build your LC.

Maybe your desire is to be in a committed romantic relationship. Check in with your LC about how many virtual love notes you can allow, receive, and accept at this very moment. Now put a tangible number of love notes to the desire. Would it take a thousand, thousands, or millions of love notes to allow, receive, and accept a committed romantic relationship? When I started my LC journey, I realized that my LOVE CAPACITY, when it came to a committed romantic relationship, was very low. My LC was populated with fear, disappointment, and sadness, which took up precious LC. Once I was able to authentically identify how many virtual love notes it would take for me to be open to the desire, I was overwhelmed with the assigned number. I started slowly, with a number that felt more comfortable, and kept increasing the number of love notes to the next level. In six months, my LC was in alignment, and I was able to allow, receive, and accept true love.

I am a huge fan of vision boards; however, over the years I would get disappointed when my visions as a whole would come up short. Today, I know that just declaring a dream or desire, without also assigning the number of virtual love notes it requires, is like trying to hit a bullseye in the dark. The worst part is that when you don't get what you want, feelings of disappointment, frustration, or anger take up precious LOVE CAPACITY.

> ...it is literally your birthright to receive massive amounts of love because you are a child of The Divine.

7/16/22
I am ready to GO FOR It!

Daily Habit - Level 1
Prayers - Pgs. 53-55 STEP 1

Level 1 - STEP 2
~~[illegible]~~
Visualization Pgs. 56-57

Level 1 - Step 3
Breathing Pg 58

Level 1 - Step 4
Stretching

Level 1 - Step 5
Journal precursors Days LC
Pg 61

# Notes / Memos

# Your Love Capacity Journey

## *It is your birthright...*

**THIS IS A REMINDER** that it is literally your birthright to receive massive amounts of love because you are a child of The Divine.

> The Divine wants you to get what you want.
>
> The Divine wants your dreams and desires to come to fruition.
>
> The Divine wants you to stand in your spotlight and share your unique gifts and talents with the world.

The best part is that by accepting massive amounts of love you honor yourself and others.

You are being of service. Yep! Did you catch that? You are literally being of service by growing your LOVE CAPACITY. As your LC grows, you will impact others around you in the best of ways. You will be more at ease and love will be a driving force in your life. That love will cross-pollinate in your personal and professional life. Because you are more at ease, people around you will be more at ease.

Because love is a driving force in your life you will be more loving and more lovable. People who are toxic in your life might find it more difficult to be around you. Just be mindful that as your

LOVE CAPACITY grows there might be shifts in relationships both personally and professionally.

Now that you have read about my Love Capacity journey and all the dreams and desires that have come to fruition to date, it is your turn. You might be asking, "Can THE SYSTEM LEVEL 1 work for me?" It can. It will. More importantly, it will—if— you make the work in this guide a priority and follow the system.

As you practice building your LC, you will be inspired to take action and to be in forward motion daily. Be sure not to skip over any step or action, hoping to find a shortcut. This guide was designed as a step-by-step system. Be sure to finish each step...in order.

The best part of the LEVEL ONE EXPAND YOUR LOVE CAPACITY DAILY HABITS—it only takes thirty minutes per day.

That is all the time you will need to invest in order to kick-start growing your LC. The other good news is that level one of the EXPAND YOUR LOVE CAPACITY DAILY HABITS SYSTEM is easy breezy to follow. I encourage you to start THE SYSTEM LEVEL 1 when you wake up—*before* you *get* out of bed—so you don't get distracted and caught up *doing* other things. I encourage you to repeat the prayers and visualization and breathing exercise laying down, to keep your body at ease. However, the most important thing is that you do the LC on a daily basis, whatever time you do it.

On your LC journey, you will find that your dreams and desires will become less of a go-and-stop process and more of a fluid journey. There will be many small and big wins that show up in tangible and non-tangible forms. At first, it will feel uncomfortable as you step onto bigger playing fields. If you continue to stay the course and do the work, what felt uncomfortable initially, will begin to feel comfortable. You will look forward to receiving more and more love.

Working within the LC SYSTEM, you will become more comfortable and aware that you are the GOLDEN CIRCLE. It is your birthright to allow, receive, and accept your dreams and desires and they are in pure alignment with your LOVE CAPACITY. Whatever you desire—whether it is money, cars, homes, business opportunities, promotions—are just love in tangible form. Rather than focus on the outcome, focus on how many virtual love notes your dreams and desire require for you to allow, receive, and accept and grow your LC to match it. The more LOVE NOTES you allow, receive, and accept the bigger your LC grows. It *really* is that simple.

Every tangible thing on earth...your dreams, desires, money, houses, business opportunities, cars, personal opportunities, a million dollars...
is just love.

# Expand Your Love Capacity Activity Section Level 1

I ASK YOU TO apply how many love notes to each dream or desire. It is important to be authentic with yourself. Then I ask you to move your dreams and desires to the side and not get caught up in any details. Instead, the objective is to build your LOVE CAPACITY daily to a Grand Canyon level.

Every tangible thing on earth…your dreams, desires, money, houses, business opportunities, cars, personal opportunities, a million dollars...is just love.

Now that you know how to go in the front door to set yourself up for success, you can grow your LC today.

Remember the memories I shared at the beginning of the book? About my boss accepting a check for one-hundred million dollars with grace and ease. Or when my friends accepted an Oscar on stage in front of millions of viewers worldwide without hesitation. Again, you might be thinking *Well, those people are famous so of course.* And I am telling you again, "It has nothing to do with fame or Hollywood. It has everything to do with their LOVE CAPACITY being big enough to allow, receive and accept massive amounts of love."

If their LC was not big enough to receive that particular dream or desire it would not have presented itself in the first place, and let's say it did present itself, something would have happened to the dream and desire from coming to full fruition. We all know the common story of people who win the lottery. Their LC was able to allow, receive, yet unable to accept, therefore they lose or spend the money and end up broke again.

I was meant to observe all that—and more—to share with you that no one is more talented or more gifted than you. They just have grown their LC big enough to match their dreams and desires. Now you have the tools to grow yours too!

# Expand Your Love Capacity Activities Section Level 1: Activity 1

## Chasing the Golden Circle

**Identify an event or** situation when you have *chased* the Golden Circle. It is important that you are mindful about how those experiences affected your choices along with how they have impacted your Love Capacity to date.

The following are examples of when someone would be *chasing* the Golden Circle. Remember when I shared how I was driving myself into the ground in pursuit of the Golden Circle via the Hollywood entertainment business? That would be one…or when someone marries into a prestigious last name and isn't in love with the person, rather, they are in love with the Golden Circle the marriage provides. Also, when someone chooses a college they can't afford…hoping that the brand name will elevate them to Golden Circle status. Staying in a relationship with a partner that makes you feel less worthy is another good example.

Not to worry, you are in great company as most people on this planet are *chasing* the Golden Circle, mostly unconsciously. The best news is that you are awakening, and I am cheering you on!

On the journaling lines that follow, take time to list events or situations in your life when you were probably chasing the Golden Circle:

___

___

___

___

# Expand Your Love Capacity Activities
## Section Level 1: Activity 2

### Defining Negative Emotions

**Now that you have** identified when you *chased* the Golden Circle, it is time to assign any negative emotions next to each experience in Activity 1. These emotions are taking up precious Love Capacity. Review the following list of negative emotions you can choose from, or you can make up your own. There is no right way to choose just as long as you authentically sit with how you felt with the outcome at the time.

#### Emotions List

Anger
Depression
Disappointment
Emptiness
Failure
Fear
Frustration
Guilt
Helplessness
Inadequacy
Jealousy
Loneliness
Negative
Overwhelmed
Resentment
Sadness
Shame

# EXPAND YOUR LOVE CAPACITY ACTIVITIES

## SECTION LEVEL 1: ACTIVITY 3

## RELEASE AND FORGIVE

**NOW THAT YOU HAVE** identified when you have *chased* the GOLDEN CIRCLE in Activity 1 and put a negative emotion next to each experience in Activity 2, it is time to forgive and release. These emotions consume precious LOVE CAPACITY. They are not serving you; they are hindering you from getting what you want. Your dreams and desires need to match your CAPACITY so take this task seriously and let yourself off the hook for good.

> I breathe in massive amounts of love today...in this very moment, and every day moving forward.

Write out the following Release and Forgiveness Love Letter and make sure to sign it.

## Release and Forgiveness Love Letter

I forgive myself the experiences I have had over the years chasing the Golden Circle. I was not aware, and I was doing the best I could. I release all negative emotions that have been taking up my precious Love Capacity. Instead, I breathe in massive amounts of love today...in this very moment, and every day moving forward. It is my birthright to allow, receive, and accept massive amounts of love. It is my birthright for my dreams and desires to come to fruition.

______________________________________

Sign Your Name Here

When you periodically feel wonky and negative emotions try to take up precious Love Capacity, please go back to your release and forgiveness love letter. Rewrite it, read it out loud, and sign it again. Also, make sure that you are consistently practicing The System: Level 1.

Now that you have released and forgiven, it is time to jump into Expand Your Love Capacity Activities Section 1 : Activity 4.

Remember when I shared the importance of dreams and desires intention setting? Well, I meant it! I just want to clarify that it is essential to get clear about each one. However, it is just as important to make sure that your LC can hold them, so do not to fill up on negative emotions.

> Do not set limitations on your dreams and desires.

# Expand Your Love Capacity Activities
## Section Level1: Activity 4

### Identifying Dreams and Desires

Get clear on what your dreams and desires are. Take your time, go for it! Do not set limitations on your dreams and desires. Since you are starting to build your Love Capacity, let's start with just three. As your LC muscle gets stronger you can add more. Write down just a couple of words that describe each one of them here:

**Create a list of your dreams and desires.**

1.________________________________________________

________________________________________________

________________________________________________

________________________________________________

________________________________________________

________________________________________________

2.________________________________________________

________________________________________________

________________________________________________

________________________________________________

________________________________________________

________________________________________________

3.________________________________________________

________________________________________________

________________________________________________

________________________________________________

________________________________________________

________________________________________________

________________________________________________

Now, set your dreams and desires to the side. Convert your dreams and desires into VIRTUAL LOVE NOTES—because money, houses, business opportunities, cars, personal opportunities, a million dollars—are just love. Every tangible thing on earth is just love.

Check in with yourself at this very moment. How many LOVE NOTES could you allow, receive, and accept? Be authentic and remember there is no shortcut. Your LOVE CAPACITY muscle will get stronger with time. However, placing the authentic amount of love notes on your dreams and desires today is important.

I want to make sure that you also know that no one grows their LC overnight. It takes time. The LC is a set of inner game disciplines that lead to outer game decisions that stretch and grow your LC and impact your personal and professional life in the best of ways.

When you achieve the initial three dreams and desires you wrote out, take time to add three more, and so on and so on. In this way, you allow your dreams and desires to keep expanding and growing.

Next is Expand Your LOVE CAPACITY DAILY HABITS SYSTEM LEVEL 1. You want to look at your LOVE CAPACITY like a muscle. The more you work it, the stronger it will get. And as it grows so will your ability to allow, receive, and accept on a massive level. Remember, the bigger the LC, the more room your dreams and desires can grow and come to fruition.

Are you ready to go for it?

Write YES here: ____________________

# Expand Your Love Capacity Daily Habits Section

## Daily Habits Level 1: Step One

*Five Minutes*

### Read These Prayers

**I had a set** of customized prayers created specifically to grow your Love Capacity and have placed them in a specific order.

The first is to reinforce that You are the Golden Circle, so you can stop chasing it.

The second is to set the tone for your day to allow, receive, and accept massive amounts of love.

The third is to be in deep gratitude for yourself and The Divine.

Recite the enclosed set of prayers out loud when you wake up in the morning and in this order.

#### The Golden Circle of Love

In this Universe, there is a Golden Circle of love. This circle is me; I am within this circle and this circle supports me. Today, as I breathe in massive amounts of love, I declare that I am filled with knowing I am worthy to receive love of all kinds and forms. Today and every day, I am aware of the overflowing capacity inside me that comes naturally and with grace, fills with love. I'm so grateful for this well inside of me that is always filling with love. I know that all I need to do is to expand my LOVE CAPACITY to allow, receive and accept my dreams and desires to come to full fruition. I accept that it is my birthright to receive the outer expression of this love in every moment of my life. My purpose is to fill the light of my star within and allow my life to reflect the truth I am a *superstar*. I allow, receive, and accept massive amounts of love every moment and all day long.

### I ALLOW, RECEIVE, AND ACCEPT MASSIVE AMOUNTS OF LOVE

Massive amounts of love surround me and are within me. I am love and love is me. At this moment, I'm aware that I'm a vessel of receiving. I'm so grateful that today this container of love is filled with lucrative ways for me to express my service through my business, experiences of success, and fame. With each word I speak and, in every moment, and without effort, I accept and participate in more of the goodness of the Universe that is my right. I can let go and allow the expansion of my receiving to increase without fear or concern. The God within me attracts the spotlight of success and fame...and I have only to express that love. I allow, receive, and accept massive amounts of love every moment and all day long.

### FOR THE DIVINE

This is the moment I pause and acknowledge the overflowing of my LOVE CAPACITY within. I know this practice of deep gratitude for myself, and The Divine acknowledges that my birthright is to receive all forms of love from the Universe. I am filled with awe at how love and The Divine are showing up in my life and breathe that truth in with thanks. I allow, receive, and accept massive amounts of love every moment and all day long.

> I am filled with awe at how love and The Divine are showing up in my life and breathe that truth in with thanks. I allow, receive, and accept massive amounts of love every moment and all day long.

# Expand Your Love Capacity Daily Habits Level 1: Step Two

*Five Minutes*

## Visualization Tool

### Expand Your Love CAPACITY WITH Cheering Crowd

**Visualization is a great** tool to grow your Love Capacity. Traditionally you might have visualized yourself solo. Today I want you to visualize a stadium full of fans who support you and cheer you on while sharing your dreams and desires with them. The cheering crowd will help you to take ownership and accountability of your dreams and desires. Allowing thousands of fans to shower you with massive amounts of love will grow your LC and may translate into the real world. Now, when you are being showered with massive amounts of love, from family, friends, colleagues, strangers…you may find yourself more at ease with it. The cheering fans will help you to allow, receive, and accept love.

Follow the step-by-step Expand Your Love Capacity With Cheering Crowd Visualization Tool

**Step #1:** Set your timer for five minutes.

**Step #2:** Close your eyes and visualize yourself standing in the middle of a large stadium full of cheering fans.

**Step #3:** Look at all the fans that have shown up for you and are cheering for you. Open your arms and allow, receive, and accept the love they are outpouring on you.

**Step #4:** Next, share one goal or desire from Expand Your Love Capacity Activities Level 1 Section, Activity 4 Section with the cheering crowd and visualize them going crazy…chanting your name…doing the wave.

**Step #5:** Now, give thanks for your LOVE CAPACITY for allowing, receiving, and accepting your dream or desire, and visualize that dream or desire in the form of virtual love notes pouring down on you from The Divine.

**Step #6:** Next, visualize your LOVE CAPACITY expanding and growing from your heart in the form of white light that spans the stadium and beyond.

**Step #7:** Finally, open your eyes when the five-minute alarm goes off and give thanks to The Divine.

**Step #5:** Repeat without interruption for five minutes straight.

> The cheering fans will help you to allow, receive, and accept love.

# EXPAND YOUR LOVE CAPACITY DAILY HABITS LEVEL 1: STEP THREE

*Five Minutes*

## BREATHING EXERCISE

It is important to release the negative emotions that had been taking up precious love capacity. Breathing in massive amounts of love is essential to growing your LC. Breathing out negative emotions is just as essential.

Follow the step-by-step LC Breathe in Massive Amounts of Love - Breathe Out Negative Emotions Exercise

**Step #1:** Set your timer for 5 Minutes.

**Step #2:** Breathe in through your nose and out through your mouth.

**Step #3:** As you breathe in through your nose, breathe in massive amounts of LOVE.

**Step #4:** As you breathe out from your mouth, release (Go back to Task 2 and pull the top three negative emotions from your list or you can breathe out the enclosed) disappointment, fear, anger.

**Step #5**: Repeat without interruption for five minutes straight.

# Expand Your Love Capacity Daily Habits Level 1: Step Four

*Five Minutes*

## Gently Stretch And Move Your Body

**Moving your body even** for a short time first thing in the morning sets you up to be more at ease in your body throughout the day. Being at ease is great for growing your LC.

It is time to get out of bed and stretch and move your body. Your body is a vessel given to you by The Divine to allow, receive, and accept love.

Gently Stretch & Move Your Body

**Step #1:** Set your timer for five minutes.

**Step #2:** Get your circulation moving and do a series of stretches of your choice.

**Step #3:** Be gentle with your vessel. This exercise is meant to awaken your vessel and get moving for the day.

Small and big wins will start to drop in because you are growing your LC. You **might want to believe** that the occurrences of these wins are random coincidences or chance opportunities...but they are not.

# Expand Your Love Capacity Daily Habits Level 1: Step Five

*Ten Minutes*

## Expand Your Love Capacity Success Notes

**Instead of writing down** the small and big Love Capacity wins at the end of your day, I want you to identify them the next day. Small and big wins will start to drop in because you are growing your LC. You might want to believe that the occurrences of these wins are random coincidences or chance opportunities...but they are not. Giving yourself time to process them is important. That is why I want you to identify them the next day. You will find yourself identifying small and big wins you may have overlooked the day before.

It is time to celebrate all of your wins so you can reference them along your LC journey.

**Expand Your Love Capacity Success Notes**

**Step #1**: Set your timer for ten minutes.

**Step #2:** Now that you have had a good night's sleep and some space from the day before, think about what your LC allowed, received, and accepted the day before. It is not uncommon that as you move through your busy day, rather than give you and your LC credit, you might refer to events as random coincidences or chance opportunities. With a fresh perspective, take the time to write down all the small and big wins.

**Step #3:** Celebrate as you catalog your wins and breathe in massive amounts of love!

## CATALOG YOUR SUCCESS NOTES

> ...when feeling conflicted, stressed, angry, jealous, or disappointed...please take a moment to breathe in massive amounts of love and breathe out the negative emotion or emotions that have bubbled up.

# Congratulations!

## *Superstar!*

**YOU HAVE COMPLETED THE** first day of daily habits the five simple steps to expand your LOVE CAPACITY. It is necessary to stress the importance of you including the steps into your daily morning routine at least Monday through Friday. You can take this next level by practicing the Expand Your Love Capacity DAILY HABITS seven days a week. However, for Level 1, five days of the week works as well.

Be gentle with yourself as you move daily from step to step. Remember, you are not brought up to take in massive amounts of love, so The SYSTEM LEVEL 1 will feel uncomfortable at first along with the results of both small and big wins that start showing up. I assure you that with time it will get easier to allow, receive, and accept love on a massive scale. As a matter of fact, you could even grow to love it so much you crave It… in the best of ways.

You are human, so there will be times that negative emotions come flooding in and take up precious LC. However, when feeling conflicted, stressed, angry, jealous, or disappointed…please take a moment to breathe in massive amounts of love and breathe out the negative emotion or emotions that have bubbled up. In fact, breathe in massive amounts of love as often as possible throughout your entire day. It is a great way to stay in alignment with The Divine and grow your LOVE CAPACITY.

> I am human and my Love Capacity Journey is a lifelong commitment. The difference is that I course correct quickly by jumping back into my LC journey...

# Love Is a Driving Force

**SINCE BEING ON MY** LC journey, you might think now that love is a driving force in my daily life, I have become a super affectionate or sentimental person. Absolutely not! I am still a bottom-liner who is not super affectionate or sentimental, nor do I care about Hallmark cards…and Halloween remains my favorite holiday.

You also might be thinking that now that I am claiming that my capacity to allow, receive and accept love and all the extraordinary things have happened both personally and professionally in my life, I don't have bad moments throughout the day or crappy days. Nope. Not at all. I have days I don't want to practice the EXPAND YOUR LOVE CAPACITY DAILY HABITS SYSTEM and I make myself do it anyway. Negative emotions start flooding my LC because someone cut me off in traffic or said something unkind to me. I get caught up in the media body shaming me or I catch myself chasing the GOLDEN CIRCLE. I am human and my LOVE CAPACITY JOURNEY is a lifelong commitment. The difference is that I course correct quickly by jumping back into my LC journey to quiet the signals, breathe out the negative emotions and allow, receive, and accept massive amounts of love. All of which puts wind beneath my wings so I can soar higher and higher once again.

Now that love is a driving force in my daily life, I know that love has everything to do with making my dreams and desires come true and I embrace it.

Today, tomorrow, and every day, I declare that I am lovable and loving. I encourage you to do the same.

## *You are lovable and loving!*

You have the inner game tools for the Love Capacity journey that will make your dreams and desires come true. Let love be your driving force.

It is your birthright to stand in your spotlight, allow, receive, and accept as much love as you can, so you can shine brightly being your own superstar.

# Your First Love Note

Dear Superstar,

So glad that we have taken this journey together. I am excited that you have said yes to growing your Love Capacity. It is your birthright to allow, receive, and accept massive amounts of love daily. It is your birthright to stand in your gorgeous spotlight and share your gifts and talents with the world. It is an honor to be of service and share my gifts and talents with you.

I send you massive amounts of love today, tomorrow, and every day!

Joie G

I am eager to hear from you, **Superstar!**

I would love to know how your expanding LOVE CAPACITY has impacted your personal or professional life or both. You can connect with me by visiting my website JoieG113.com. You can also connect with me on social media: Facebook, LinkedIn, and Instagram.

https://113branding.com/
https://www.facebook
https://www.linkedin.com/in/joiegharrity/.com/JoieGharrity
https://www.instagram.com/joiegharrity/

# Sincere Gratitude

### Berta Nunez-Gharrity—

Thank you for your support and encouragement to always follow my dreams and to never define myself by other people's standards. You inspire me daily to smile, stay positive, embrace my purpose, stand in my spotlight, and shine bright.
Proud to be your daughter.
Love you more!

### Roger Moore—

Thank you for your love, unwavering support, and encouragement for me to stand in my spotlight and share my gifts and talents with the world. You are the wind underneath my wings and because of our union, I am soaring higher and higher.
Love you, sweetie.

### Raquel Gharrity—

Proud to be your big sister. Your creative talents have always inspired me to stretch and expand my creativity. Your courage to put your creative vision out in the world is empowering and powerful.

Go, sister, go!

**Gavin Gharrity—**

I loved being your big sister. Your love and support to go for it especially while we worked in the Hollywood entertainment business were priceless. Your support and love on the other side make my heart sing. I will continue to look for pennies you send me from heaven.

Love you, sweet brother!

**Sheila Kennedy—**

Sister, your encouragement to become an author and write my first book, *The Red Carpet Guide to Visibility and Influence* was a game-changer. It is because of you I am in forward motion and making my dream come true with my second book. You are the ultimate mentor and publisher.

Thank you so much!

**Betty Withrow—**

I appreciate you so very much. Thank you for being an amazing book coach. Your guidance was on point and your encouragement was exactly what I needed to keep going no matter what.

Sending you love, Sister!

### Jennifer Urezzio—

You are a master prayer maker. Thank you for creating the customized prayers for the Expand Your Love Capacity Daily Habits System. Your gifts and talents for putting words to my downloads and gratitude for The Divine are a blessing.
Thank you, sweet Sister!

### Heather Leineweber Robison—

Thank you for sharing your gifts and talents with me once again. I am grateful for your book cover design that created a gorgeous spotlight for me to stand in. You are a superstar!

### Roland Emmerich—

Your mentorship was a gift. Your ability to allow, receive and accept your dreams to come to full fruition made a huge impact on me.
Thank you so much!

## Paula Allen—

When I reached out and asked for your support you immediately said yes. When I showed you the direction, I wanted to take the book marketing campaign you immediately got it. I thank you for showing up big for my vision sister.
You are a Rockstar!

## Claudine Francois—

You were the first to request to learn more about Being Your Own Superstar—How to Expand Your Love Capacity. Your enthusiasm gave me the courage to stay in forward motion no matter what. I am grateful for your gorgeous testimonials and support.
Thank you so very much!

## Jeff Vinokour—

Your generosity of spirit literally changed the course of my life. Opening doors to a career in the Hollywood entertainment business took me on an exciting journey and stretched me both personally and professionally. Your continued support over the years means the world to me.
Thank you, sweet friend!

## Lisa Pagan—

Sister, when things were dark, and the tunnel was long, your advice and friendship were front and center. I thank you for your unwavering friendship and support. When I jumped a cliff and launched my live event series you were the first to buy a ticket and attend. Seeing you in the audience took the experience next level. Thank you so much.
Sending you love, sister!

## Hamilton and Lamar—

Thank you for making me your sister. Your brotherhood has meant so much to me over the years. Being part of your family is fabulously chic.
Sending you gems and diamonds!

## Mary Turner—

Everyone needs a Mary T in their life! Your advice and support are always spot on. Your enthusiasm for life is contagious.
Sending you love!

## Ron Goeschi—

Thank you for your support and love over the years. You have a big heart and a beautiful spirit sweet friend.
Grateful for you!

## Stacy Bloodworth—

So glad we are sisters. Thank you for sharing your creative gifts and talents with me and the world. You are a superstar.
Sending you hearts!

## Gina Estrada—

Your friendship was a tipping point in my life. Your confidence in me and my talents elevated my vision and belief in myself. Your courage inspires me daily. Thank you for encouraging me to get louder. Thank you for being my angel.
Sending you massive amounts of love!

## Anna Weber—

Your years of expertise in book formatting have made my book shine. Thank you for being a master at your craft!
So appreciative of you!

## Mark Pedowitz—

Thank you for giving me the opportunity to shine bright. Your support and encouragement gave me the courage to swing for the stars. I am grateful for your mentorship.
Thank you so very much!

## Frank Bennett Gonzalez—

Over the years your friendship has meant the world to me. Thank you for all your support and for always seeing me and celebrating my talents.
Thank you, Brother!

## Caren Glasser—

Thank you for encouraging me to step out of the shadows and into my spotlight. Your generosity of spirit is one of the many reasons I am a big fan of yours.
Grateful for you, Sister!

## Ross Brand—

So glad we were connected and share the same enthusiasm for Livestream and the online world. Look forward to spotlighting and celebrating talent globally.
Thank you, Brother!

## Mark Netter and Peter Rafelson—

Thank you for inviting me to join the ElectraCast family. You both are visionaries with big hearts.
Cheers to you, Brothers!

Louis Casillas—
You are the best big brother a girl could ask for. Thank you for sharing your wisdom with me over the years.
Sending you love, Brother!

Susan Jacobs—
Grateful we became instant sisters that day we spent exploring San Francisco together. Your friendship means the world to me.
You are beautiful both inside and out, Sister!

Sylvia Bambra—
You are one of the kindest people I know, Sister. Your continued support and encouragement mean the world to me. Thank you for standing next to me during the bad and good times.
I appreciate you, Sister!

Jennifer Dorian Shepherd—
Your time and wisdom are much appreciated. Your feedback elevated the project in the best of ways.
Thank you so much, Sister!

# Being Your Own Superstar
Joie Gharrity

# About Author Joie Gharrity

**JOIE GHARRITY, FOUNDER OF** Joie G 113, is a Brand Director, Author, Livestream Host, and International Speaker. She worked in the Hollywood entertainment industry for fifteen plus years at top companies, in film, television, original web content, and branded entertainment. She was hand-picked by the ABC Studio President to launch the first multi-media startup business for The Walt Disney Company.

After returning to the Bay Area, Joie was inspired to launch Joie G 113, where she works with entrepreneurs and creative types to leverage their expertise, gifts, and talents. She integrates her visibility strategies, tools, and tips that lead to greater influence along with both the creative and business sides of the entertainment industry through her unique, tested, and proven 113 SUPERSTAR VISIBILITY AND INFLUENCE SYSTEM. Her system includes inner game tools, which she has coined the EXPAND YOUR LOVE CAPACITY DAILY HABITS. Her unique approach elevates her clients to superstar status in the marketplace.

Joie gets you on the red carpet with her first book, *The Red Carpet Guide to Visibility and Influence.* She shares her Hollywood journey along with branding and marketing techniques used to turn up the spotlight on your personal and professional brand to grow your visibility and influence and increase your earning power. Now that you are on the Red Carpet, Joie's second book, *Being Your Own Superstar: How to Expand Your Love Capacity*, gets you on the big screen by focusing on your inner game. Joie observed superstars and leaders in the industry while working in Hollywood and has discovered their secret sauce. The size of their LOVE CAPACITY is in direct alignment with how large of a spotlight they can stand in, and how much love they are able to allow, receive and accept from the marketplace.

Joie shares her signature journey to being her own superstar along with techniques, tools, and tips that will enable you to take your LOVE CAPACITY to superstar status, push through the glass ceiling, replace overwhelm with eagerness and focus, and become a superstar in your life. She designed the book to double as a play guide for you to implement her signature program, EXPAND YOUR LOVE CAPACITY DAILY HABITS, to manifest your dreams and desires quickly and easily.

Gharrity also launched *The Hollywood Spotlight Series,* a live interview show that features industry influencers. Guests share tools and tips on how they took their dreams from conception to fruition. The intention of the show is to inspire everyone to DREAM BIG and TAKE INSPIRED ACTION. She also launched *Being Your Own Superstar,* another live interview show that features leaders in their field. Leaders share strategies and tips with the marketplace about how they have grown their LOVE CAPACITY, which has taken their personal and professional brand to the next level. Both shows double as organic commercials as Joie artfully spotlights her guests' books, products, services, movies, web series, and more.

Joie truly believes that it is your birthright to stand in your spotlight and shine bright and that it has nothing to do with the last name you were born into or your vocation. ---Instead, it is living your true purpose, turning up your VISIBILITY SPOTLIGHT, growing your Influence and allowing, receiving, and accepting massive amounts of love.

Made in USA - Kendallville, IN
33330_9781735163895
03.16.2022 1432